SO-DVE-732

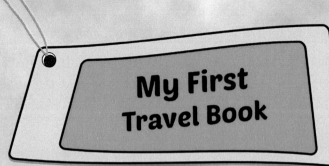

My First
Travel Book

This book belongs to:

....

From:

....

Date:

....

Signed by:

....

My First Travel Book

with
Captain
Frankie

Anna Othitis

My First Travel Book

Illustrations by Cleoward Sy

Cover Design by Cecelia Morgan

Formatting by LionheART Publishing House, part of LionheART Galleries Ltd

A special thank you to my son, Frankie Othitis, "Captain Frankie".

He is a pilot and has provided me with the inspiration and encouragement to author children's books. It is a pleasure to create this wonderful series of *My First Travel Books* with more adventurous travels on our amazing "Angelic Airlines".

To my husband, George, and sons, Johnny and Elia, thank you for your wonderful encouragement, inspiration, praise and support at all times. You are all such shining stars of love and affection in my life.

Of course a big thank you to my wonderful little readers for your support and expressive imaginations.

Thank You All So Much

Welcome aboard Angelic Airlines. This is your Captain Frankie, and I will be flying you to some of the most popular destinations around the world.

Please fasten your seat belts, stow your bags, make yourselves comfortable and get ready for a smooth take off on a wondrous journey into the deep blue skies.

Beautiful Colorful Country Flags of Our World

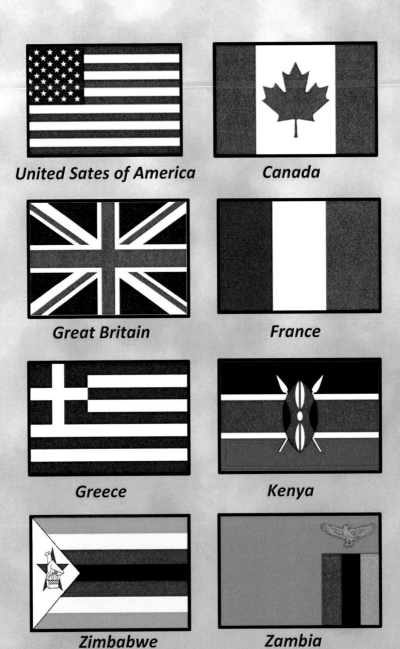

United Sates of America

Canada

Great Britain

France

Greece

Kenya

Zimbabwe

Zambia

This is a map of our world which shows where you can find our amazing attractions.

What a big world we live in, so wide and spread over the oceans.

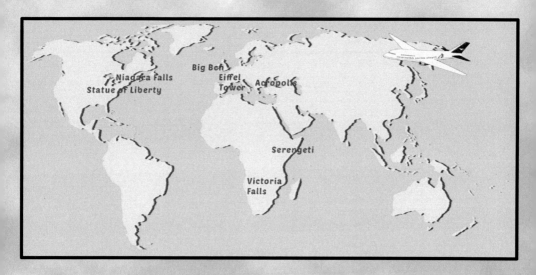

Statue of Liberty: New York, USA

A torch she holds high, she stands on a star,

a crown on her head, she stares out so far.

To all who can see her from miles away,

she will send the message she sends every day.

That is to let the whole world know

of the life, liberty and happiness her country will show.

Our first destination will be the wonderful United States of America. Out of the fifty different states, our first sight to see is the Statue of Liberty—an amazing symbol of America's freedom.

The Statue of Liberty is more than a statue. She is a beloved friend, a living sign of freedom. She can be found in New York City.

In her left hand, she holds an important book which measures as long as a minivan and as thick as a wall. Written on the book is the American Independence date, the fourth of July. In her other hand she holds the bright torch that shows the path to a land of freedom.

Where is the Statue of Liberty?

Why did they build the statue?

Why was she built?

What does the Statue of Liberty hold in her left arm?

Niagara Falls: USA and Canada

Like a curtain of water that falls to the ground,

thousands of gallons roar to make a thundering sound.

As amazing as it is to the people that see,

Niagara Falls is a wonderful place to be.

Our next exciting destination is not too far from the Statue of Liberty. Pay attention, children, as we fly over this wonder of nature.

Get ready to see the amazing Niagara Falls. Together they are some of the largest falls in the world which creates a border between America and Canada.

The water comes from the Great Lakes which are Lake Superior, Lake Ontario, Lake Michigan, Lake Erie and Lake Huron.

Most of this thunderous water meets here and then runs from the lakes, over the Niagara Falls.

Where are the Niagara Falls?

Which countries share the Niagara Falls?

Why the Niagara Falls different waterfalls?

Big Ben: London, England

Tick tock, tick tock, the hands sweep around the clock,

listen very carefully and you may just hear the sound.

From the River Thames and the great big London Eye,

you can hear Big Ben play its chime as the hour goes by.

I am so excited! Our next trip takes us to the biggest clock in the world and can be reached by going up 334 steps.

The famous clock can be found at the north end of the Palace of Westminster in downtown London.

The clock's arms are kept swinging by the pendulum below which is weighed down by stacks of coins.

When Parliament meets, a light above Big Ben is switched on to let the people know.

Where is Big Ben?

Why is the clock so popular?

What keeps the clock arm swinging accurately?

Eiffel Tower: Paris, France

Excuse moi, s'il vouz plait,

off to Paris, France to spend the day.

Like a gigantic rocket in the sky,

the Eiffel Tower stands alone,

an enormous iron beanstalk that's fully grown.

This old steel structure used to be a watch tower during the war and attracts many people from around the world, and now you get to see it!

Sit back, relax, and enjoy the flight to the 1050 foot Eiffel Tower, about the same height as an eighty-one story building.

So bright she shines in the middle of the night.

In which country is the Eiffel Tower?

Why did they build the Eiffel tower?

What did they build the Eiffel tower with?

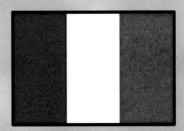

Acropolis: Athens, Greece

The Acropolis was built high on a mountain
so strong and true,

for the ancient Greeks to look out
to the Mediterranean Sea so blue.

The Greek Gods called it home,
and could go there to meet and talk,

and today it is a famous tourist attraction
for people to go admire and walk.

The Acropolis has many different temples, which were built by the ancient Greeks with great big pillars and marble floors.

The Acropolis was used as a hiding place and a lookout for enemies.

Down below are the big old stone, open-air theaters, which are still used for famous outside plays and music concerts where the people rejoice in dance and song.

In which city is the Acropolis?

Who built this big temple?

Why did the ancient Greeks build the Acropolis?

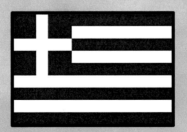

Serengeti: Kenya

Lions, elephants, zebras and snakes,

live in Africa's jungles, rivers and lakes.

The Serengeti safari, a once in a lifetime sight,

keep your hands and feet inside

some of the wild animals might bite.

The Serengeti Park is located in Kenya, Africa and is famous for the many wild animals that live there and it is the largest, free, and natural wildlife park in the world.

The park has millions of different kinds of wild animals and birds. The Maasai African tribal people still live close by, in their own villages in hut homes built so strong.

Where is the Serengeti?

In which country and continent is the Serengeti?

*Name some of the wild African animals
that live in this game park.*

Victoria Falls:

Zimbabwe and Zambia, Africa

Under the African sun the Victoria Falls stand
a famous landmark to the Zimbabwean land.
Looking mighty and sounding so strong,
look how it stretches so far along.

Did you know that the Zambezi River, along with the three hundred and thirty foot drop waterfall, creates the border between Zimbabwe and Zambia?

The water eventually runs into the Zambezi River and into the Indian Ocean.

The African people call the Victoria Falls "The Smoke that Thunders," and this is because the water crashing to the bottom makes such a loud rumble, almost like an earthquake.

The spray that the water makes can also be seen from miles away, along with a very colorful rainbow.

Which countries share the Victoria Falls?

What does Victoria Falls mean?

Into which ocean do the falls run?

In which continent is the Victoria Falls?

Captain Frankie's Quiz Question

Children, can you remember which sights we have been to visit?

Speak them out loud with me:

The Statue of Liberty

Niagara Falls

Big Ben

Eiffel Tower

Acropolis

Serengeti

Victoria Falls

Girls and boys, this brings us to the end of our amazing travels around the world. I hope that you had a fun and pleasant flight. I thank you for flying with me, your Captain Frankie, on Angelic Airlines.

We got to see and learn about some of the most amazing attractions on our earth. I hope to see you all again very soon and we always welcome you aboard.

More Angelic Airline Adventures coming soon,

with your friendly Captain Frankie

"We Are The World, We Are The People Living In It"

Children, here is your boarding pass and airplane ticket for Our Next World Travel

SEE YOU SOON!

Made in the USA
San Bernardino, CA
28 June 2016